Bandanna

Paul Muldoon, who was born in Northern Ireland in 1951, is the Howard G. B. Clark Professor in the Humanities at Princeton University.

Bandana, with music by Daron Aric Hagen, was commissioned by the College Bands Directors National Association.

PAUL MULDOON

Bandanna

An opera in two acts
and a prologue

faber and faber

First published in 1999
by Faber and Faber Limited
3 Queen Square London WC1N 3AU

Photoset by Wilmaset Ltd, Wirral
Printed and bound in Great Britain by
Mackays of Chatham plc, Chatham, Kent

© Paul Muldoon, 1999

Paul Muldoon is hereby identified as author of this
work in accordance with Section 77 of the Copyright,
Designs and Patents Act 1988

A CIP record for this book
is available from the British Library

ISBN 0-571-19762-0

2 4 6 8 10 9 7 5 3 1

In memory of Olivia Kuenne (1991–1997)
and Britt Arvid Hagen (1957–1997)

Dramatis Personae

Morales Tenor
The Latino chief of police of a tiny town
on the border of the US and Mexico.

Jake Baritone
Morales' white lieutenant.

Cassidy Bass Baritone
Morales' Irish–American captain.

Mona Soprano
Morales' white wife.

Kane Dramatic Baritone
A labor organizer.

Emily Lyric Mezzo-soprano
Jake's Latino fiancée and
Mona's best friend.

A Young Mexican Girl Mute

Mixed Chorus of illegal immigrants, townspeople, migrant
workers, wedding guests, the 'dispossessed' and the
'disappeared'.

On-stage Mariachi Band of from four to ten musicians,
including a **Guitar Player**, who play a combination of
notated and improvised parts.

Prologue

House lights up. A highly stylized projection on to a scrim of onion fields. The chorus of the Dispossessed and the Disappeared remains backstage, amplified.

Dispossessed
Dona nobis requiem.
To live is to sleep.
To die is to awaken.

*Llegaramos de solapo
entre dos aguas.
Dona nobis requiem.*

The house lights dim. The onion-field projection dissolves. Police cruiser lights roll in. A ghastly pulsating red. Fade. November, 1968. A moonless night. A desert. An irrigation ditch, all the way up a steeply raked stage, from which sixteen illegal immigrants are crawling. They are naked, save for their underwear. Each carries before him, like a badly wrapped gift, a cellophane bag containing his few possessions, including a skeleton costume and mask associated with the Day of the Dead, which they don as they sing. The ghostly percussion of a Mariachi Band.

Illegal Immigrants
We struck out across the mesas,
the canyons and arroyos,
for days and days.
We saw the ghosts of Cabeza
De Vaca and Benito Juarez
along the way.

We snuck out along the mesillas
and fenced-off coulées
crawling with watchdogs and warders.
We came on Santa Anna and Pancho Villa
where some gulch or gully
made a mad dash for the border.

Leader
I've led them across the Rio Grande
to the milk and honey of the Promised Land.

Illegal Immigrants
We strike out across the river,
plastic bags between our teeth.
We know what it's like to hover
between life and death.
We move like shades between the two
in the desperate hope of breaking through.

*There follows a brief spoken call and response between the
Leader and the rest of the Illegal Immigrants.*

Through thick and thin,
dona nobis requiem.
By hook or by crook,
dona nobis requiem.
Come hell or high water,
dona nobis requiem.

In a nick of time,
dona nobis requiem.
For better or worse,
dona nobis requiem.
Over our dead bodies,
dona nobis requiem.

Illegal Immigrants
Over the Rio Bravo del Norte
we carried our earthly goods.

One time in the Sierra Madre
we came on the ghost of Cortés.
He unwound his ragged hood
and he said, '*Mis compadres*,

as you swim across the river
with your lives between your teeth,
you know what it's like to hover
between life and death,
moving like shades between the two
in the hope against hope of breaking through

to the mile-high other side of the mile-wide Rio Grande
where death hath no more dominion.
It's a peerless Promised Land
whose arroyos and canyons
are filled not with sand
but milk, *mis compadres*, and onions...'

We snuck among the sleeping hosts—
the barrios, the auto-wrecks.
We knew we were near the border
when we came on Woodrow Wilson's ghost.
He was manning his little border post.

Leader
'I just want to check,'
Señor Woodrow says, 'that your papers are in order...'

*A uniformed and armed Jake has emerged from stage left,
carrying a heavy flashlight. He plays the light over the
otherworldly faces of the Illegal Immigrants, till it comes to
rest on the Leader. The percussion stops abruptly. A moment
of uncertainty.*

Leader
(*Spoken:*) San Joaquín...

*Jake shakes the Leader's hands, embraces him, a general
sense of relief as they slap backs.*

Illegal Immigrants

We struck out across the river,
plastic bags between our teeth.
We know what it's like to hover
between life and death.
We've moved like shades between the two
until now, at last, we've broken through.

Act One

The scrim rises and the lights come up suddenly on the main street of a tiny town. The sets are minimal throughout. Some are flown in. The essence of the design is understatement: the reverse of a neon motel sign conjures up a motel; a cantina stage right is summoned up by a few stools, another neon sign and the archetypical swinging doors. The Illegal Immigrants, ushered into the scene by Jake, are swallowed up by a skeleton-costumed and masked throng of Townspeople celebrating the Day of the Dead. The Mariachi Band is now playing at full tilt, accompanied only by percussion in the orchestra.

Townspeople
You've been carried across
the threshold of pain.
It's as if you've forced
through some flimsy membrane.
For better or worse
you've come to life again

Where the living and dead go hand in hand
to the rhythm of a mariachi band
on the Day of the Dead,
Dia de los Muertos,
when the living break bread
with Coronado and Cortés.
The lines of which you were once so sure
begin to blur
on the Day of the Dead.

Jake pauses to kiss Emily, who turns to confide in Mona,
who wears a distinctive red bandanna.

Emily

Oh, Mona. I'm suddenly less than clear
about my feelings for Jake.

Mona

               Emily, my dear,
you win a man over to your side
and the things that were cut and dried
seem less so. A man will overstep the mark...

Emily

I reached out to him in the dark
last night and ran my hand along a spine
of dark...

Mona

          You have to draw a line...
Has he ... forced ... you again?

Emily

Oh, Mona ... A flimsy membrane...

Emily has been selecting onions from a stall. She clasps them
to her breast but they fall.

Santa Maria ... Santa Anna...

Mona

Please, Emily ... Take my bandanna...

Mona takes off her bandanna and gives it to Emily, who
wraps the onions in it.

Townspeople

The things that were once clear
are suddenly thrown
out of whack, out of gear.
We enter the zone

where the distant is all too near
and the dead come into their own

on the Day of the Dead,
Dia de los Muertos,
when the living break bread
with Coronado and Cortés.
The lines that once seemed so secure
begin to blur
on the Day of the Dead.

*Mona and Emily lead us to the door of the cantina, which
Jake is about to enter.*

Jake

They say the border is a state of mind.
I think that's a little bit ill-defined.
It's real enough to *mis compadres*
who hoof it over the Sierra Madre
for days on end. That's real enough.
They hoof it over the basins and bluffs,
the mesas and the valleys,
only to be caught red-handed by Morales
and his new *Capitan* ... Captain Cassidy.

*Jake gestures towards Cassidy, who's at the bar of the
cantina with Kane.*

Morales made him captain over me
though I was next in line. I'll pay
Morales back one of these fine days.

Jake enters the cantina.

Townspeople

When you fall in with our parade
the line between what's true
and false begins to fade.
You're caught between the two

like a shade between two shades
and you know in your heart you'll rue

the Day of the Dead,
Dia de los Muertos,
when the living break bread
with Coronado and Cortés.
Everything that looked like it must endure
begins to blur
on the Day of the Dead.

Cassidy takes a swig from the bottle of beer Kane has bought for him. He studies the bottle.

Cassidy

These greasy wetbacks seem to find
that a slice of lemon rind
makes this horse-piss taste better.
Life or death? It doesn't matter
to them. They don't care if they snuff
it at forty. That's why they drink this stuff

down in Tequila Alley.
I'm now the right hand man to Morales.
His new *Capitan* ... Captain Cassidy.
I have to overlook the fact that he's
a greaseball himself. I look the other way.
I guess that every dago has his day.

Cassidy takes another swig, slumps at the bar.

Townspeople

We set plates of little marzipan skulls
by our family graves
on the Day of the Dead. All was null
and void as the ground gave
way beneath us. Our senses grew dull.
It seemed that the living must save

the Day of the Dead,
Dia de los Muertos,
when the living break bread
with Coronado and Cortés.
Everything that said 'As you were'
seems to blur
on the Day of the Dead.

Kane props Cassidy at the bar, then moves out of earshot.

Kane
Cassidy must be out of his mind
if he thinks James Kane would stand for this kind
of anti-Mexican patter.
I'll fill him full of fire-water
and use him to get to Morales. He's so tough,
Morales, when he's putting handcuffs
on my workers. It seems that I'm their sole ally
when they've been handcuffed by Morales
for holding so-called 'illegal assemblies'.
Morales and his new *Capitan*, Captain Cassidy
locking up my workers in the land of the free.
Miguel Morales won't always hold sway.
I'll settle his hash one of these fine days.

Kane joins Cassidy by the bar.

Cassidy
When will you ever learn to unwind,
Citizen Kane?

Kane
When Morales has resigned
as Chief of Police.

Jake approaches Cassidy.

Jake
Your aider and abettor.
Your partner in crime.

Cassidy
Bean-eater.

Kane
Boys, boys, boys.

As Emily and Mona approach, Kane eyes Mona.

Nice little muff.

Jake
I wouldn't mind seeing her in the buff.

Cassidy
You'll be found dead in an alley
if you lay a hand on Mona Morales...

Jake
And you'll have to deal with *me*
if you mess with little Miss Emily.

Kane
You watch your step, Jake. Some people say
you're working both sides of the street, night and day.

*There follows a Trio based on the solos by Jake, Cassidy and
Kane, with occasional interjections from the Townspeople
drawn from the dialogue between them. At the conclusion of
the Trio, Kane accosts Jake in a stage whisper.*

Some say that the real Saint Jack
has less time for wetbacks than greenbacks.
He spends time in an irrigation ditch
because he needs the money to get hitched.

*Jake takes a swing at Kane, misses him, hits Cassidy. A
melée involves the entire chorus of Townspeople. Cassidy*

draws his police revolver, begins to pistol-whip Jake. Kane, meanwhile, has managed to slip away. A police cruiser sweeps in, bringing with it Morales.

Morales

Why do they have to let me down
in front of my own town?

There's an almost immediate return to order. Morales points to Cassidy, now joined by Emily and Mona.

Captain Cassidy's under arrest.
I'm relieving him of his duties.

Cassidy is led away. Morales turns to Jake, bloodied on the ground.

That Jake has put my patience to the test
once too often.

To Mona and Emily:

Home, my beauties,
before things go from bad to worse.

To the Townspeople:

I'll give you one minute to disperse.

The Townspeople pick up Jake and carry him out.

Townspeople

Let none of you tarry
on your way home
to the barrio
or you might just become
a dead man's quarry.
When you meet a dead man,
knife to knife,
one on one,
however much you lunge and parry

and cry out for dear life,
you know in your bones
that the dead will carry

the Day of the Dead,
Dia de los Muertos,
when the living break bread
with Coronado and Cortés.
The things that seemed so firmly moored
begin to stir
on the Day of the Dead.

SCENE 2

*As the neon signs and cantina doors are flown out, twin
picket fences, front doors and couches are flown in. A lone
Guitar Player is left onstage from the previous scene,
improvising a folk tune for his own amusement. Jake is
carried through his front door, laid on a couch, where he is
attended by Emily and Mona. Morales, meanwhile, stands
by his front door, clearly dejected.*

Morales
Why do they have to let me down,
Jake and Cassidy,
in front of my own town?
Have they no respect for me?

They've spent *Dia de los Muertos*
drinking beer and wine
with Coronado and Cortés
while I put myself on the line

again and again
where a neon sign
leaves a little stain
on the desert air,

where a worked-out mine
continues in that vein,
where a flowering vine
is rooted in Spain,
where the earth's so bare
it hides for shame,
and it's there, *mis compadres*, there
I put myself on the line.

For them and for those other fools,
those other burros,
who think Montezuma still rules
the canyons and arroyos

I do feel some tenderness.
I still get a shiver down my spine
when the Border Patrol or the INS
catches them crossing the line

again and again,
for how little we divine
of what a *bracero* hopes to gain
when he dares
to climb a high-voltage line
so as to drain
power enough to shine
a light on his pot of plantains.
He sends up a flare.
A spout of flame.
I try to imagine the despair, the despair
that's put him there on the line.

Cassidy is like my own son.
A flame I fanned from a spark.
But when Cassidy draws a gun
he oversteps the mark.

For the law's the law
come rain or shine.
And once Cassidy draws
he puts me in the firing line

again and again
as when we drank rice wine
and smoked a few grains
of opium on that fateful R and R.
I still see the cardboard sign
that read 'My name is Jane.'
I still feel the nub of her spine
through the flimsy counterpane.
I didn't know why Cassidy would try to tear
the J from her name
as she whispered 'There, my darling, there.'
She was strangling him with a fishing-line.

As for Jake, I'm quite convinced
he's out every night
cutting holes in a chain-link fence
to shed a little more light

on the Lone Star state.
When he stands between two piñon pines
and opens the flood-gate
and starts to feed me that line

again and again
about how we must refine
the 'sacred' and 'profane'
into something rich and rare,
how we must combine
their separate strains
so they intertwine
into one thick skein,
that there's some design
we can easily explain,

that all will be fine
if we only sustain
our belief in the divine,
that we'd see beyond the pain
of the God hanging there
and invoke his name –
then and only then might we have a prayer
of getting things back in line.

And Mona? I rushed back from town
to be with my own little beauty.
She knows I'd let her down
over my dead body.
How I miss my little sweet.
For she and I know intimately
what it is to resign
ourselves to some no-man's-land.
I hang on a high-voltage wire.
I reach out to her across the DMZ
as fire reaches out to fire.
Between swaddling band and winding sheet
we put our necks on the line.
For we put our heads in a noose
when it comes to those we love.
Though she once played fast and loose
with Sergio Limón – I beat him into juice,
I washed him down the sluice –
though she once played fast and loose,
when push comes to shove
I pledge myself to Mona,
my fountainhead, the wellspring I divine
in this no-man's-land, this *zona
media*, my little bride of the borderline.

*Mona has made her way from Jake's bedside, where he's
now sitting up, still tended by Emily, who has wrapped his*

head in the distinctive red bandanna. Mona embraces
Morales.

Mona

Miguel, you've been gone so long.
I've been waiting for you
to come back from town
like the girl in that old song
who sings of her true
love and lets her willow-hair down.
For the alder and the willow
nail their colors to their masts.
The hearts on their sleeves
are stuck through with a knife.
An alder cannot help but bend
out of some deep sense of shame.
A willow will quiver and quake
in a wind, however slight,
since it's doomed to eternal unrest.

Mona moves towards Morales. They embrace.

Morales

I forgive you your peccadillo.
I believe it's a thing of the past.
As I hope you firmly believe
in my love for you, dear wife.
An alder cannot help but tend
towards a river bed, much the same
as a willow tends to a lake.
I love you, Mona, not despite
but because of your fouling our nest.

*Morales and Mona sing a Duet based on the above. Emily
has been helping Jake out of bed. As he dresses, she comes to
the front door.*

Emily

When I reached out across my pillow
last night and the night before last
there was only dark. How can a man deceive
his wife-to-be? The rumors are rife.
He's been seen twice along the Big Bend
coming out of a house of ill-fame.
If only Emiliano Zapata, my namesake,
might come to my aid, if only he might
lay his head on my breast.

*Jake has now made his way towards Emily, taking off the
distinctive red bandanna, folding it, putting it in his pocket.*

Jake

As I drove between Canutillo
and Smeltertown last week, real fast,
with a load of Mexican chicken-thieves
I suddenly hated my double life.
Yet those illegal immigrants who wend
their way north, who know my name
not as Lieutenant Lopez, not as Jake,
but San Joaquín – their plight
has put my love for Emily to the test.

*There follows a Quartet based on the above. As Mona and
Morales go inside, hand in hand, Emily reaches out to Jake,
who shrugs her off. Emily goes inside as Jake is left alone. He
carries a bottle of tequila.*

Jake

I know that I've been gone too long
and that you, Emily, you
are waiting for me to come back to town
like the girl in that old song
who sings of her true
love and lets her willow-hair down.
Donde esta mi querido?

Mi charca esta quieta.
Nuestro amor ha tenido una vida corte.
Mi sauce esta delgado.

In El Paso once I saw her skirt billow
out like Marilyn's from the blast
of a hot-air vent. I knew I'd cleave
to her. I'd take her to be my wife.
Last week Morales asked me how I spend
my nights. I came up with some lame
alibi. I know he knows it was fake.
I know he'll wait till his case is watertight
to issue a warrant for my arrest.

Jake looks back wistfully to his house.

Donde esta mi querido?
Mi charca esta quieta.
Nuestro amor ha tenido una vida corte.
Mi sauce esta delgado.

I'll risk one last run to Amarillo
before I quit. Even if his case is iron-cast,
Morales would give me a reprieve
because he likes to twist the knife.
I feel bad that Mona and Emily are friends
but I have to beat Morales at his own game.

Jake takes the bandanna from his pocket, unfolds it, then
slowly tightens it around his forearm like a tourniquet.

Maybe I'll find a use for this little keepsake.
Maybe then Morales will remember his birthright.
Maybe he'll remember that he, too, was dispossessed.

An instrumental segue as the houses and fences are flown out. An eerie zone, a liminal place, a place of 'ghostlier demarcations'. Jake moves away, putting the bandanna in his hip pocket, as Kane, also carrying a bottle of tequila, enters from the up-stage area associated with the irrigation ditch. They circle as if they might at any moment attack each other.

Kane

I'm sorry, Jake. I didn't mean for it to end
in blood and tears.

Jake
End?
What makes you think it's over?

Kane

You must have one hell of a hangover.

Jake

One I'm no more likely to forget
than I'm likely to forget
the man who gave it to me.

Kane
    Cassidy?

Jake

The very one. *Capitan* Cassidy.
I'll settle his hash one of these...

Kane

      ...fine days?
Isn't that what those Americanos say?
Sounds to me like you're in a rut.
You're stuck in a groove.
But you know in your gut

you've got to make your move.
You've spent too much time in an irrigation ditch
trying to find your own little niche.

*Kane offers Jake a drink of tequila. Jake declines, preferring
to drink from his own bottle.*

Jake

The worm in this bottle ... See ...
The bastard's got his eye on me ...

Jake mops his brow with the bandanna.

Kane

You're heading for the onion fields?

Jake

No. Should I be?

Kane

It's just that the onion fields
are sprayed with DDT.

Jake

DDT ... DDT ... Isn't that what the crickets sang
as we plodded up the beach at Danang?

Kane

DDT. It lies on the ground like manna.
My workers wear bandannas
to keep from breathing in
the poison.

Jake

Your workers?

Kane

Through thick and thin
I stand by them.

Jake
You sound like Davy Crockett.

Kane
Not General Antonio Lopez de Santa Anna?

Jake
This red and white bandanna
doesn't come from the hip-pocket
of one of your onion-pickers, Kane...

Kane reaches out and takes the bandanna from Jake.

Kane
This does look like an onion stain.

Jake
It comes from the lily-white neck
of Mona Morales...

Kane
I think of how my workers trek
across the mesas and valleys
only to end up in another rut.

They're stuck in another groove.
They know in their guts
they've got to make their move.

Jake takes another drink of tequila, studies the bottle once again.

Jake
Little worm. Lily-white one.
Why so tightly curled?
Must you atone
for the sins of the world?

Gusañito. Little snake
gorged on fusel oil.

White as arsenic.
Why do you recoil?

Kane

When all is said and done,
Jake, our plot has unfurled
como la rosa sobre el rodrigon,
la raiz en realidad.

Kane muses on the bandanna.

We should be able to take
our enemies in this toil.
For this red rose is staked
in reality's soil.

Kane and Jake sing a Duet based on the above. Jake is clearly incoherent, mesmerized by the worm in the bottle.

Jake

Little bud of manna.
Little Aaron's rod.
You cut such a dash.
Little sword of God.

Little captain's stripe.
Victor of every affray.
Little white-as-ash.
Why do you look away?

Kane returns the bandanna to Jake, who shuffles off.

Kane

We'll use that bandanna
as a snare. We'll use it to prod
Morales. He'll think his white trash
wife's having her sod

bust by Cassidy. The time's ripe
to make them pay

the price. I'll settle their hash
this finest of fine days.

SCENE 4

Lights down. Kane strides forcefully down-stage into a spot.
The projection of onion fields. An onion truck.

Kane
I think, *mis braceros*, of how you trek
through Laredo and El Paso
only to put your neck
on the line for a few pesos.

I think, *mis braceros*, of how you flood
across the mile-wide Rio Bravo
only to end up sweating blood
for a few lousy centavos.

Another day, another dollar,
hitch your wagon to a star—
isn't that the American way?
They put your neck in a collar.
They hooked you to a tool-bar.
They hitched you, *mis braceros*, to the clay.

The time has come to make a stand
in what was held out as the Promised Land
whose arroyos and canyons
are filled with milk, *mis braceros*, and unions.
Now I hear the angels' wings . . .
Now I hear the angels sing,

'Off the hook, all you who grub
through lemon groves and onion fields,
all you who stand and rub
your eyes . . . Now, all shall be revealed . . .

For, if you organize,
there's a chance you might yet rise
above the harrows, the rollers,
another day, another dolor,
past the campfires where you cook,
over all that's overlooked...
There's a chance you might steer clear
of this endless vale of tears...
There's a chance you might get off the hook.'

Through thick and thin
I've always stood up for you.
You're like my own kin.
I want always to be true

to the vision I held out
when you grovelled in slime.
It seems I wiped your snouts
in a nick of time.

I'm appalled by how they abuse
los conquistadors de Kane.
You have nothing to lose,
mis braceros, but your chains.

Marx, of course, is out of favor today
because of the Commie thing.
When Kosygin calls for LBJ
he hears that red phone ring

off the hook ... All you who grub
through lemon groves and onion fields,
all you who stand and rub
your eyes ... Now, all shall be revealed...

*Kane steps over to the running-board of the onion truck,
showing his true feelings.*

However much these greasers organize
they'll never rise
above the onion fields' red clay.
They much prefer to stay
In their stinking little huts.
They've been too long in the sun.
You can smell them for miles.
And when all's said and done
they love to be reviled.
They like their little groove.
They settle where they settle.
They like their little rut.
They'll never make the move.
They're pigs ... Pigs or cattle...
That side of beef ... That bacon flitch...
I love to see them twist and twitch.

Kane resumes his grandiloquent pose.

In a nick of time,
mis braceros, you left Mexico.
Now there's quicklime
everywhere you go.

There's blood on the stones
everywhere you look.
The police are breaking bones
by hook or by crook.

As I look through the flimsy curtain
into this world, *muchachos*,
a world in which nothing is certain
but death and, maybe, Texas,

I'm sure the self-same Uncle Sam
who lets us take a swing
through Cambodia or Nam
will never let the Kennedys or Martin Luther King

off the hook ... All you who grub
through lemon groves and onion fields,
all you who stand and rub
your eyes ... Now, all shall be revealed...

Kane again steps up to the running-board of the onion truck.

However much these greasers organize
they'll never rise
to the occasion ... Come what may,
they're *mestizos* – that's to say
'mongrels' or 'mutts'.
They still pray to the sun
like they did in the wild.
Their idea of fun
is to sacrifice a child.
On the Day of the Dead it behooves
them to worship Quetzalcoatl
or some shithead. They cut
off bits of flesh as the spirit moves
them, shaking their rattles
and dancing at such a pitch
their own mothers can't tell which mutt's which.

Kane resumes his grandiloquent pose.

By hook or by crook,
you've managed to break through,
though when Mao wrote the book
he wasn't thinking of you.

I admire the steadfastness
with which, *mis braceros*,
you've flown in the face of the INS
for better or worse.

I think, *mis braceros*, of how you've stood
firm since you banded

together. There's now much less likelihood
of your being caught red-handed

by *La Migra*, though your hands are red
and your eyes sting
as you drag onions from their beds
or cut down onions, string upon string,

off the hook . . .

*The lights come up to reveal a chorus of Migrant Workers,
who enter carrying great strings of onions which they place
in baskets.*

Migrant Workers
All of us who grub
through lemon groves and onion fields,
all of us who stand and rub
our eyes . . . Now, all shall be revealed . . .
For, if we organize,
there's a chance we might yet rise
above the harrows, the rollers,
another day, another dolor,
past the campfires where we cook,
over all that's overlooked . . .
There's a chance we might steer clear
of this endless vale of tears . . .
There's a chance we might get off the hook.

*A flashing light from a police cruiser. A squad of police in
riot gear, led by Morales and Jake, herds the crowd to one
side.*

Morales
To live is to sleep,
to die is to awaken?
You've lived like sheep.
You'll die like chickens.

Kane

What have we here, *mis amigos?*
The slaughter-yards
of Chicago? Where's the tear gas?
Where's Daley? Where's the National Guard?

Morales

I'll give you and your *pollos*
one minute to disperse
before I send in my police.

Kane

Your police, Morales?

Morales

       I'm not averse
to arresting the rooster.

Kane extends his arms, daring Morales to handcuff him.

Kane

Your police or mine?

Morales

I'll have you for a feather duster
if you cross the police line . . .

A stand-off ensues. The leader of the group of Illegal Immigrants, now a Migrant Worker, approaches Jake.

Leader

(*Spoken:*) San Joaquín.

A moment of recognition. Jake pushes the Leader away, pretending not to know him. Too late. Morales now knows that Jake is involved in bringing in illegal immigrants.

Morales

Arrest that sheep . . . And check
that the others' papers are in order.
Arrest that sheep, Jake . . .

I know you're a prince among sheep-herders...
You can watch your chickens wing
it all the way to Singsing...

*Jake moves disconsolately among the Migrant Workers,
arresting two or three, sending the others off. They sing as
they disperse.*

Migrant Workers
Off the hook? All of us who grubbed
through lemon groves and onion fields,
all of us who stood and rubbed
our eyes ... Now, all is indeed revealed...
For, though we organize,
there's no chance we'll ever rise
above the harrows, the rollers,
another day, another dolor,
past the campfires where we cook,
over all that's overlooked...
There's no chance we'll steer clear
of this endless vale of tears...
There's no chance we'll get off the hook.

*As the last of the Migrant Workers disperse, Jake and
Morales are left alone.*

Jake
I'm sorry, Miguel. I didn't mean for it to end
in blood and tears.

Morales
I'm sorry, my friend.
I'm sorry to embarrass
you in front of your sorry-ass
chickens. Especially sorry, I guess I am,
after all we went through together in Vietnam.
Something snapped in you there, Jake.

Jake steps up to the running-board of the truck to give an aside.

Jake
Listen to this shithead, for pity's sake.
Something 'snapped'? I can hear the 'sickening thud'.
Now I know he's after my blood.
Now I'm forced to screw him over.

Jake approaches Morales with fake concern.

I'm sorry to hear it might be over
between yourself and your *media naranja.*

Morales
You're poisonous, Jake. You make Agent Orange
seem like a cure.

Jake
I like a man who's secure
in himself. It's touching
that you don't mind Cassidy touching
her up.

Morales
You were too long in Cambodia.

Jake
You know how she spent *Dia
de los Muertos*, your better half?

Morales draws his pistol.

I'm telling you this, Miguel,
out of a son's sense of duty
to his father. I feel honor-bound...

Morales
Honor? You go to hell...
Don't give me that rooty-tooty...
You lousy, lying hound...

30

Jake

I'm concerned about your better half . . .

Morales

I've half
a mind to settle your . . .

Jake produces the bandanna with a flourish.

Jake

Why don't you settle the hash
of the man from whom I got this sash?

Morales

Sounds to me like you're in a rut.
You're stuck in a groove.

Jake

Cassidy was grabbing Mona's butt.
He was putting the moves
on her.

Morales

Who's paying you to turn snitch?
Would it be Comrade Kanovitch?

Jake

This bandanna comes from the lily-white neck
of . . .

Morales

I don't care if it comes from the lily-white neck
of Madame Mao Zedong
or Madame Chiang Kai-shek.
You spent too much time along the Mekong.

Now you act like you're a god.
You act like you're divine
because you were in a Daniel Boone squad
and went behind enemy-lines

again and again,
where the mountain inclined
towards the plain
as if it might care,
where they intertwined
in a shower of rain,
anti-personnel mines
among the razor-sharp canes,
the rabbit snare
attached to same,
and the stare, Jake, the wounded stare
of Cassidy hooked by a fishing-line.

Jake

We stepped through the flimsy veil,
you, Cassidy and myself.
We learned to live beyond the pale.
We mastered life-in-death.

It was there that we honed our art.
There it was refined.
It earned Cassidy a purple heart.
I learned never to toe the line

again and again
where a naval ensign
would flutter in vain
for support from the air,
where the sirens whined
along a baggage-train,
we fired our carbines
out of pure disdain,
and we all must share
the blame, Miguel, the blame
for strapping that gook to a bamboo chair
and shooting him point-blank...

Morales puts the pistol to Jake's head.

Morales

It's the end of the line
for you. You'll buy the ranch
if I hear any more shit about my half-orange.

*Morales sends Jake sloping off at gunpoint. Unbeknownst to
Morales, Jake lingers by the running-board of the onion
truck. Morales muses on the bandanna.*

Mother of God.

For better or worse
I must see this through.
Little lure of lures.
Little love lasso.

Little trip-wire
on the field of slaughter.
Little flash of fire
come hell or high water.

Come hell or high water
you're the little flag
at half-mast on a cutter.
Little gag. Little snag.

Little red rag
I gave my little beauty.
She'll go on a jag
over my dead body.

However much I want not to believe my eyes
I have to remember the lies
she's told me. She's already strayed
from the fold. Why does she have to betray
me in front of my own town like a ewe in rut?
And with Cassidy? He's been like a son
to me. He's been like a child.
I feel like I've been done

33

a great wrong. I've been reviled.
If it turns out that there's any truth
in what that worm in the bottle
has to say, I'll kill the slut.
If it turns out Jake's telling the truth,
I'll put an end to all the prattle.
I'll pull the plug. I'll throw the switch.
It'll be curtains for that bitch.

Act Two

A riot of excitement in the cantina, where Jake and Emily's wedding reception is in full swing. The neon sign fairly throbs, despite lacking its M. The Mariachi Band excels itself as a chorus of Wedding Guests dance and sing exuberantly.

Women Guests
A man shows his true feelings
at a wedding feast.
When a man's done with reeling
off his vows to the priest
and comes away a groom
only then does he guess
at the vast wilderness
of the bridal room.
He throws his eyes to the ceiling
and howls like a beast.

Men Guests
A woman shows her true feelings
at a wedding feast
when her wheeling and dealing
have, for the moment, ceased
and the position she assumes
as she pauses to assess
the cut of her dress
and her little h'm-h'ms
means she knows she's most revealing
when she reveals least.

Wedding Guests

We show our true feelings on a wedding day
because we know it must give way

to the night, the night of love,
la noche de la boda,
when push comes to shove
and our dead bodies
that have so long lain hidden
in the gulches, the gullies,
the fenced-off coulées,
will rouse themselves, unbidden,
for a night of love.

*Morales drains a bottle and steps forward to deliver a toast
to an ecstatic Emily, a slightly subdued Jake. Morales is
somewhat the worse for wear. His tone is appropriately
askew.*

Morales

For better or worse
let us drink to Emily and Jake
and the wee small hours
when they will partake
of a sweetness as fierce
as the sweetest wedding cake.

For richer or poorer
I raise a glass
to the boy from the barrio
who managed to pass
through the barbed-wire barriers
between class and class.

In sickness and in health
I sing a paean
to the girl who raised herself
above her fellow peons.

They wallow in filth.
She shines like neon.

*The Wedding Guests look askance. They give Morales a
wide berth as he lurches in their midst.*

May every joy, or its sad ghost,
that's buried in the heart
now do its utmost
to stir and start
and join with me in this toast
till death us do part.

Here's mud in the eye
of the girl from Amarillo.
To live is to sleep.
To die is to awaken.
May Emily and Jake's
cups of wine run over.

Morales sings pointedly to Mona.

May they wake to find the joy
I thought would be mine
with my own little beauty
for ever, ever more.

*A Sextet of Morales, Emily, Jake, Mona, Cassidy and Kane
as they raise their glasses. This is followed by a waltz based
on 'Donde esta mi querida?', in which Jake and Emily are
featured.*

Emily

I turn from the sky
like a weeping willow
and ponder the deep.
When I think of San Joaquín
my heart no longer aches.
I'm no more in a fever.

What I feel for that bit of a boy
for whom I once would pine
now has a sense of duty
at its core.

A pasodoble featuring Mona and Morales to the 'Alder and
willow' *tune.*

Jake

It used to be I would fly
between Canutillo
and Smeltertown with my load of sheep
or chickens.
No headlights. No brakes.
Those days are over.
No more chicken-convoys.
But again and again I think of Madeline
and Rosa and Jane and Betty
and Eleanor.

A beguine featuring Morales and Emily to the 'Again and
again' *tune.*

Mona

Sometimes I want to curl up and die.
I know I shouldn't wallow
in self-pity but woes just heap
themselves on me. I'm stricken
with grief to think he might mistake
my motives. We'll never recover
from the Limón thing. It's going to destroy
our marriage. The taste of turpentine.
I know I shouldn't wallow in self-pity.
Little running sore.

Jake sweeps Mona away in a traditional tango based on the
'Little worm' *theme, throughout which Kane has been
making advances to a Young Girl.*

Cassidy

It's the mark of Kane. Look at him ply
that poor child with tequila.
You can see the poison seep
out of him. My heart sickens
when I see him take
advantage of her. When he endeavours
with his little ploys
to hook her on his line
he forgets that *she*'s the jail-bait
writhing on the floor.

A 50s rock dance based on the 'Off the hook' *theme in which
Kane and the Young Girl are featured.*

Kane

I lurk like a spy
round the gibbet and the gallows.
It's my job to keep
things on the boil. The plot thickens.
I give it a stir. Morales will take
Mona and Cassidy for lovers
because I had that shithead Jake deploy
the thin red line
of a bandanna. Little spotty-wotty.
Little noose. Trap-door.

*A samba featuring Cassidy, whom Jake has steered into the
arms of an initially reluctant, if increasingly responsive,
Mona, who places a marigold between her teeth.*

Wedding Guests

When Cassidy strikes out across the sawdust
the floor will give way beneath
him and, though he'll try to readjust
his red neckerchief,
it'll be too late. There'll be nothing he can do.
He'll be caught in a lasso.

And when Mona strikes out across the sand,
a marigold between her teeth
it'll come not from a bridal garland
but her own funeral wreath,
for Miguel Morales will think it true
that she's taken Cassidy in her arms with a view

to a night, a night of love,
la noce de la boda,
when push comes to shove
and our dead bodies
that have so long lain hidden
in the gulches, the gullies,
the fenced-off coulées,
will rouse themselves, unbidden,
for a night of love.

Morales is enraged by the display of affection between Mona and Cassidy.

Morales

Now I know it was all a lie.
She's as shallow
as her own grave. Her talk's as cheap
as herself. Again and again
I've watched her make
eyes at other men ... Share her favors.
There's nothing so coy
as a coy concubine.
She's a prostitute ... *Una puta.*
A dirty, stinking whore.

A stunned silence. Morales lurches towards Mona, who disappears, followed by Cassidy, as the Wedding Guests close in. Emily weeps uncontrollably. Morales slouches off.

Wedding Guests

How can he let himself down
like that, how can he let himself appear
to be some kind of clown
just because Cassidy got too near
to his little half-orange, Mona?
How she must wish
that some great fish
would swallow her as it swallowed Jonah
and bear her out of town
like a body on a bier.

SCENE 2

*The liminal zone. Kane is left with the Young Girl. They are
seated side by side on a bale of hay. Kane drapes his arm
across her shoulder. She turns away, shrugging off his arm,
but does not get up.*

Kane

Why do you shrink
from Señor Kane?
Why should a link
deny its chain?

He traces a finger down between her breasts.

Is that some sort of charm
between your breasts?

She draws away.

Why don't you rest
your head in my arms,
lily-white one, lest
you come to harm?

41

He addresses the audience directly:

Why would a drain
shy away from its stink?

He turns back to the Young Girl, tracing a line along her throat.

Across the bridge
that hangs between poverty and privilege

let me lead the way, lily-white one,
oh so tightly furled,
across the bridge of bones
into the liminal zone,
into the other world.
Under the arch, along the stays,
across the span
of a finger and thumb splayed like a fan,
let me lead the way
across the bridge of bones.

Jovancita. Let me take
you down the back alley
along which I led Jake
and Cassidy and Morales.

The Young Girl is now somewhat attentive.

Those three cottonwoods
mistook a sewer for a stream.

Little buttress. Little beam.
I've only just understood
I hit upon that scheme
simply because I could,

She is now quite smitten.

because Miguel Morales
and Cassidy and Jake

let me lead the way, lily-white one,
oh so tightly furled,
across the bridge of bones
into the liminal zone,
into the other world.

He traces a line from her fingertip, along her arm, to her chin.

Under the arch, along the stays,
across the span
of a finger and thumb splayed like a fan,
they let me lead the way
across the bridge of bones.

Kane tilts her face towards him, as if he might kiss her.

Now I see you look to Señor Kane
as if you might bring balm to his bane...

Kane holds her chin with one hand. With the other, he traces a line across her breast, over her belly, and beyond.

Asclepias mexicana.
Little milkweed pod
on which no monarchs flash.
I recognize that nod.
How did you get that rash?
Little guttersnipe.

Kane now pushes her away.

I know your type.
You'll want me to pay
in the hardest cash.
Just like Maria and Ella May
and Martha and Maud
and Mona and Marianna

who would have let me lead the way, lily-white ones,
all so tightly furled,
across the bridges of their bones
into the liminal zone,
into the other world.
I don't want to seem arch, but I never stay
when things have gone according to plan
and, for the simple reason that I can,
I'll be making my merry way
across the bridge of bones.

Kane moves off, leaving a bewildered Young Girl.

SCENE 3

Night. The reverse of the neon motel sign, minus its M, and the cantina. Jake enters, is served a beer, reads a paper. A flown-in door and window suggest a mean room. A mussed-up bed. The ghastly flickering of a television screen facing downstage. Mona enters, evidently perplexed, bolts the door behind her, checks the window, draws the curtain.

Mona
Three long weeks I've lain low among
these molds and mildews
in the saddest part of town.
Though I've done no wrong
I have to keep out of view
because Miguel's vowed to cut down

this beautiful, long-haired willow
who's been outcast
on the world ... It makes me believe
that the afterlife
is here and now. I've seen the end
of life as it was. But I'll die game.

44

How could Miguel mistake
me for some lady of the night
when it's my honor he's transgressed?

*Mona checks outside, opens the door to Emily, who enters
and begins to unpack a paper sack of groceries topped with a
string of onions and a bunch of marigolds.*

Emily
I'm sorry to have taken so long
but I couldn't get through
from the other side of town.
There was such a throng
at the corner of Brazos and New
because of some police shake-down.

Jake waved at me with his night-stick
and called to me in a voice all muddy and thick

*Donde esta mi querida?
Mi charca esta quieta.
Nuestro amor ha tenido una vida corte.
Mi sauce esta delgado.*

Emily pauses to savor the marigolds.

The scent of marigolds. *Las maravillas.*
The wonder would be if we outlast
these flowers that people leave
on graves. Marigolds. Loosestrife.
Now that Mona must spend
her days under an assumed name
I feel like someone who brings tacos and Tastycakes
to her grave on All Souls' Night
so she'll have something she can digest.

Mona
Oh, Emily, you've been such a pillar
of strength.

Emily

Is that a caterpillar
on the onions?

Mona

Thank God you've been able
to put some food on my table.
Again and again you've managed to slip
behind enemy lines and give Miguel the slip.

Emily

You know, Mona, that I dote
on you...

Mona

You're the perfect antidote
to the venom I can all but see
around me.

Emily

Just the same with the VC,
according to Jake ... Same in Nam.

Mona

When will I find *requiem aeternam*?

Emily

The only hope you have of keeping your skin whole
is by staying in this fox-hole
until Miguel recognizes his own good fortune
and changes his tune,

Emily puts her arm around Mona.

till the alder sees the willow
as being quite steadfast
after all ... On the Eve of All Hallows
I've stood on the edge of a vast
pit and heard the dead grieve
for the passing of a girl to a midwife.

Into a midwife's hands they commend
each girl's spirit. They blow on the flame
of each of us, give us a slap and a shake
and consign us, Mona, to our earthly plight
in which, however distressed,
we must learn to sit tight
and wait till our men are once more self-possessed.

Mona
Till the alder sees the willow
as being quite steadfast
after all? The gibbet and the gallows
could not look more aghast
than Miguel looks at me. I'm hardly so naïve
as to think our marital strife
might soon be over. It's hard to mend
such a mile-wide rift. Nor can I blame
poor Miguel for wanting to rake
over the embers, Emily, of every slight
real or imagined ... The best
I can hope for is that he'll see the light
that glows for him within my ashen breast.

Mona and Emily sing a duet based on the above.

Emily
When I saw Jake at the corner of Brazos and New
I immediately wanted to renew
my wedding vows.

Mona
Is he still off the force?

Emily
Miguel fired him. I've no idea what force
might have led us both there.

She glances at her watch.

I promised to meet
him at five in the cantina.

Mona
I'd be dead meat
if I came face-to-face with the wraith
who stalks me.

Emily
I think the force was faith.

Mona
Fate or faith?

Emily
Same thing. You have to trust
in something beyond yourself.

Mona
The knife aspires to rust,
I know, just as a strip of cloth
yearns for the moth.
The crib is a crypt, the cot a catacomb.
These marigolds have made a tomb
of a moldering motel room.
When can I break out of it? When can I go home?

Emily
Not yet, Mona. You have to stay put.

Mona
Must I stay *la puta*?

Emily
Miguel was overheard
last week at the firing range
saying he offered a reward
to the man who brought him his 'rotten half-orange'
dead or alive.

Mona

You should go, Emily. It's 10.05.

Emily busies herself to leave.

Do you think you might ask Brother Odilo
to bring me communion? I'll fast
and pray till All Hallows' Eve.
I'll defend myself not with a two-edged knife
but a breastplate of faith. Faith will defend
me from Miguel. I see him take aim
at me again and again. Why should I break
out of one tomb only to fall right
into another? I must wear my faith like a bullet-proof
    vest.

*Mona kneels by her bedside to pray silently as Emily makes
her way out and across the street to the cantina. Jake and she
embrace.*

Mona

To die is to awaken
and come into bud
as the willow quickens
in the willow mud.

We come into bud
and put out a shoot.
In the willow mud
we put out a root.

We put out a shoot
at the moment we die.
We put out a root
and sing a lullaby.

At the moment we die
the dead are sent

to sing a lullaby
instead of a lament.

The dead are sent
to twist, all night long,
instead of a lament
a cradle song.

They twine all night long
through the deep dark
a cradle song
from a single spark.

Through the deep dark
they pleat and plait
from a single spark
a basket of light.

They pleat and plait
and lay down tenderly
a basket of light
by the foot of a tree.

They lay down tenderly
as a body would set
by the foot of a tree
a mud-spattered bassinet.

As a body would set
by the river edge
the mud-spattered bassinet
of their own ribcage,

by the river edge
I beat my breast,
my own ribcage,
that I may be blest.

I beat my breast
since the dead hold sway.

That I may be blest
I kneel to pray.

Since the dead hold sway,
as some suppose,
I kneel and pray
to Almighty God. Who knows

if, as some suppose,
we've been forsaken
by God, albeit a God who knows
that to die is to awaken?

Mona gets into bed, laying the marigolds on her own breast.
Morales crosses to the motel, forces an entry to the motel
room, closing the door behind him. He takes the bandanna
from his pocket and fashions it into a noose. There follows a
garish pantomime in which Morales strangles Mona. She puts
up a feeble struggle but manages a cry. Jake and Emily hear
the cry, cross towards the motel. Mona dies. Morales is
suddenly paralysed with horror. He hears Jake enter behind
him, pivots, fires blindly, hits Jake, who goes down. Emily
rushes in, throws herself on Jake's lifeless body.

Morales

Looking into the sky:

Again and again
I've asked them to fix that sign.
It looks strange without the M.

He turns to Mona.

How I miss my own little beauty.

He contemplates the bandanna.

Winding-sheet. Swaddling-band.
She knows I'd let her down
over my dead body.

He realizes the burden of what's happened.

Holy Mother of God.

Morales puts the pistol to his mouth and fires. As the shot rings out, Emily screams. The orchestral percussion takes over, becoming deafening as a chorus of Paramedics, Townspeople, the Dispossessed and the Disappeared streams onstage. Slow Curtain.

Chorus

She struck out across the river,
marigolds upon her breast.
She blew on *las maravillas*
so that they were blest.
She unsettled their little petals
with her own last breath.

She unsettled those marigolds
as she met their cold with a greater cold.
As her winding-sheet turns into a swaddling-band
she's one with the communion
of saints who move through the land.
These arroyos and canyons
are filled not with sand
but the souls, *mis amados*, of our old companions.

To live is to sleep,
to die is to awaken.
Dona nobis requiem.
To live is to sleep,
to die is to awaken.
Dona nobis requiem.
To live is to sleep,
to die is to awaken.
Dona nobis pacem.